THE ULTIMATE BRAIN BENDER

ACTIVITY BOOK

THE ULTIMATE BRAIN BENDER

ACTIVITY BOOK

JOE RHATIGAN ILLUSTRATIONS BY ANTHONY OWSLEY

MoonDance

Brimming with creative inspiration, how-to projects, and useful information to enrich your everyday life, Quarto Knows is a favorite destination for those pursuing their interests and passions. Visit our site and dig deeper with our books into your area of interest: Quarto Creates, Quarto Cooks, Quarto Homes, Quarto Lives, Quarto Drives, Quarto Explores, Quarto Gifts, or Quarto Kids.

First Published in 2017 by MoonDance Press, an imprint of The Quarto Group.
26391 Crown Valley Parkway, Suite 220, Mission Viejo, CA 92691, USA.
T (949) 380-7510 F (949) 380-7575 www.QuartoKnows.com

MoonDance Press titles are also available at discount for retail, wholesale, promotional, and bulk purchase. For details, contact the Special Sales Manager by email at specialsales @quarto.com or by mail at The Quarto Group, Attn: Special Sales Manager, 100 Cummings Center, Suite 265D, Beverly, MA 01915, USA.

ISBN: 978-1-63322-162-8

Design & page layout: Melissa Gerber

Printed in China
10 9 8 7 6 5

THIS BOOK WILL HELP YOU MATCH YOUR SOCKS!

Life is full of challenges. For some of you, the simple act of waking up on time can seem an impossibility. Then there's finding a matching pair of socks and then locating your shoes before the school bus shows up. These challenges are a drag. So, we filled a whole book with **fun** challenges and dares. With just a pencil and your brain (if you can find it), you can take on one or more of the dozens of "brain benders" in this book. Can you draw 50 cats in a living room? Of course you can! Can you draw a maze around its solution? Yes! Can you find nine-letter words trapped in a box? We certainly hope so! From completing proverbs, drawing strings on a stringless harp, and reading mixed-up words to drawing a bicycle from memory and solving crossword puzzles without enough clues, these challenges will keep you thinking and moving. Pretty soon, you'll be great at taking on any challenge that comes your way!

And when you're all grown up with all sorts of grown-up challenges, you'll remember this book and say, "*The Ultimate Brain Bender Activity Book* helped me match my socks."

Oh, there it is.

THE BICYCLE TEST

A psychologist investigating how we recognize everyday objects asked more than 200 people to draw a bicycle without looking at one. Her results: Many people have no understanding of how bicycles work. Can you draw a 10-speed bicycle (or multi-speed mountain bike) without looking at one? *See page 140 for images.*

Can you draw a bicycle built for two?

How about a tricycle?

IT ALL ADDS UP

Can you place the numbers 1 through 19 in the circles below so that each row of three circles equals 22? A few numbers are already in place to help you out. **Answers on page 140.**

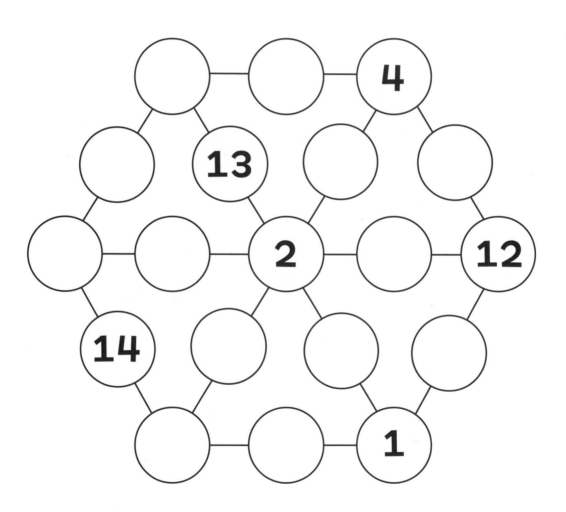

This one is more difficult. Can you place the numbers 1 through 19 in the circles below so that each of the rows and diagonals end up equaling 38? Unlike the previous puzzle, you need to add the full row or diagonal—follow the lines between circles. *Answers on page 140.*

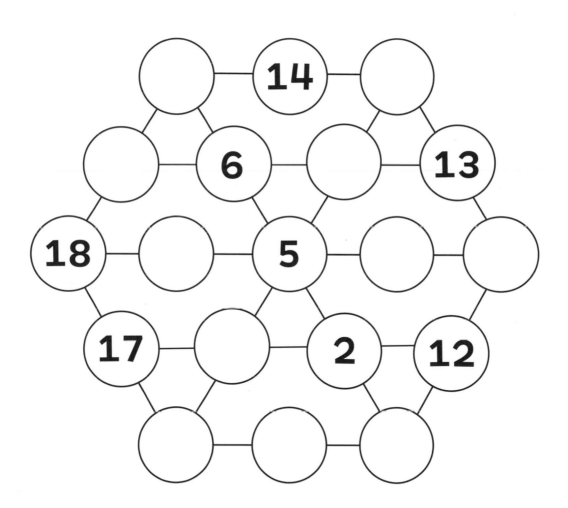

LEFTY/RIGHTY

Can you sign your name with your non-writing hand?

Can you draw this elephant with your non-writing hand?

Can you decipher the coded messages on the next few pages using the unfinished code grid below? You will have to fill in the grid as you decipher the messages! **Answers on page 140.**

	A	B	C	D	E	F	G	H	I	J	K	L	M	N	O	P	Q	R	S	T	U	V	W	X	Y	Z
1														■												
2																							■			
3																										
4																										
5																										
6																										
7																										
8																■										
9			■																							
10										■																
11																										
12		■																								
13												■														
14							■																			
15																					■					
16		■																								
17																								■		
18																		■								
19																										
20																										
21																										
22																										
23																						■				
24					■																					
25									■																	
26																										

A) __ __ __ __ __ __ __ __ __ __ __ __ __ __ __ __ __
   3   4 5 2 4 6 7   26 21 19 15 14 21 26   4 3 18

__ __ __ __ __ __ __ ... __ __ __ __ __ __ __
 2 4 7   24 18 20 20   15 1 26 3 5   3

__ __ __ __ __ __ __ __ __ __ __ __ __ __ __ __ __ __.
16 19 15 14 21 26   4   16 4 14   19 24   12 21 3 8 7

B) __ __ __ __ __ __ __ __ __ __ __ __ __ __ __ __ __
   4 9 15 5 26 7   4 18 20   10 15 7 26   25 3 9 7

__ __ __ __ __ __ __ __ __ __.
 2 3 26 21   13 19 1 20 6

C) __ __ __'__ __ __ __ __ __ __ __ __ __ __ __ __
   6 19 15 18 20   7 19   19 5 9   26 21 4 26

__ __ __ __ __ __ __ __ __ __ __ __ __ __ __ __,
 2 21 20 1   6 19 15   2 20 18 20   4   25 3 9

__ __ __ __ __ __ __ __ __ __ __ __ __
26 21 20   9 20 4 9   7 20 4   2 4 7

__ __ __ __ __ __ __ __!
19 1 5 6   7 3 12 25

D) __ __ __ __ __ __ __ __ __ __ ; __ __ __ __ __ __ __ __

16 20   6 19 15 18   7 20 5 24   20 23 20 18 6 19 1 20

__ __ __ __   __ __   __ __ __ __ __ __ __   __ __ __ __ __ .

20 5 7 20   3 7   4 5 18 20 4 9 6   26 4 25 20 1

E) __ __ __   __ __   __ __ __ __   __ __ __ __

2 21 6   9 19   12 19 2 7   2 20 4 18

__ __ __ __ __ ?   __ __ __ __ __   __ __ __ __ __

16 20 5 5 7   26 21 20 3 18   21 19 18 1 7

__ __ __ ' __   __ __ __ __ .

9 19 1 26   2 19 18 25

F) __ __ __   __ __ __ __ __ __ __ __   __ __ __ __ __ ?

12 4 1   24 20 16 18 15 4 18 6   13 4 18 12 21?

__ __ , __ __ __ __   __ __ __ __ __   __ __ __ .

1 19   16 15 26   4 8 18 3 5   13 4 6

G) __ __ __ __   __ __ __ __ __   __ __ __   __ __ __ __

2 21 4 26   2 19 15 5 9   6 19 15   12 4 5 5

__ __ __   __ __ __ __ __   __ __   __ __ __ __ __ __ __

26 21 20   12 21 3 5 9   19 24   4 23 4 13 8 3 18 20

__ __ __   __   __ __ __ __ __ __ __ ?

4 1 9   4   7 1 19 2 13 4 1

__ __ __ __ __ __ __ __ !

24 18 19 7 26 16 3 26 20

PIXELATION

Can you draw the following items by filling
in the boxes on these pages?

House, Dog, Tree, Woman, Man, Elephant, Truck, Skyscraper,
Lamp, Guitar. . . and whatever else you can think of.

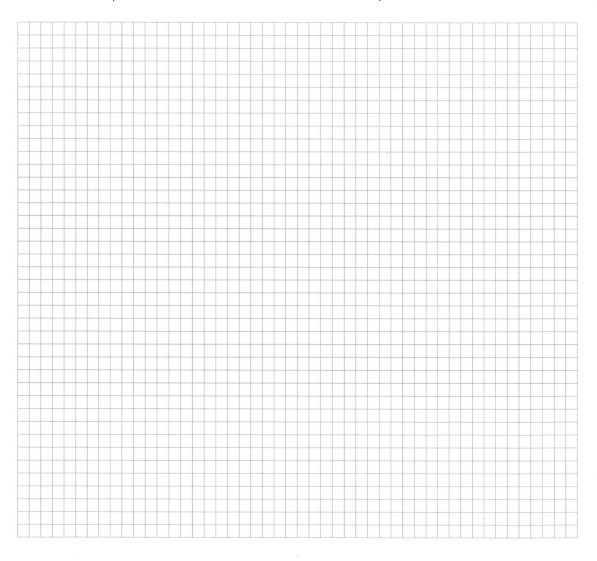

Can you fill the fridge with a week's worth of groceries?

SIX ANSWERS, THREE CLUES

Can you figure out how these crossword puzzles work?
Answers on page 140.

Clues

1. # of days in a week
2. What you use to talk
3. The daughter of one's brother or sister

Clues

1. Tired of the same old same old
2. Rhymes with "time"
3. What your brain does at night

Clues

1. What you watch on a big screen
2. This person parks your car
3. More than usual

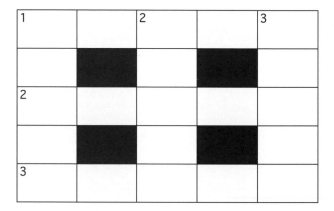

Can you solve this one without any clues?

This one has even fewer clues.

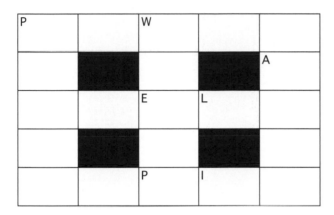

Now, create your own and see if a friend can figure it out.

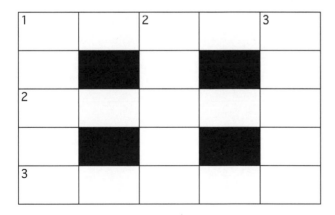

MIX & MATCH

Can you connect these illustrations so they spell out six-letter words? To make this a little more challenging, the answers are mixed in with the clues. For example: If there were an illustration of an eye and of a lid, that would spell "eyelid." On the page you would find an illustration of an eye, some sort of lid, and an eyelid. Each image is used only once. **Answers on page 140.**

THIS
END
UP

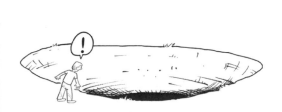

FAST FLICKS

Can you come up with at least 25 different movie titles in three minutes? To make it a game, have someone else do the same thing. Then compare lists and cross out any movies you have in common. The person with the most movies left over, wins.

1. _____

2. _____

3. _____

4. _____

5. _____

6. _____

7. _____

8. _____

9. _____

10. _____

11. _____

12. _____

13. _____

14. _____

15. _____

16. _____

17. _____

18. _____

19. _____

20. _____

21. _____

22. _____

23. _____

24. _____

25. _____

Here's a page for your friend:

1. _____

2. _____

3. _____

4. _____

5. _____

6. _____

7. _____

8. _____

9. _____

10. _____

11. _____

12. _____

13. _____

14. _____

15. _____

16. _____

17. _____

18. _____

19. _____

20. _____

21. _____

22. _____

23. _____

24. _____

25. _____

X MARKS THE SPOTS

Can you place an X in six different squares in the grid below so that there is only one X in each row, column, and diagonal?
Answer on page 141.

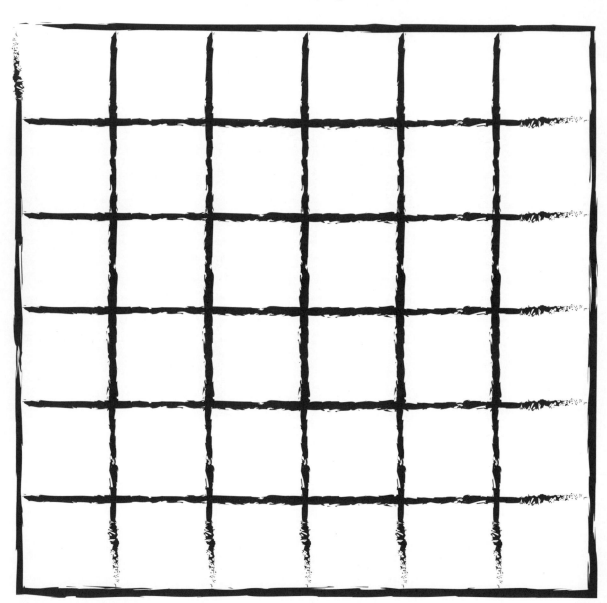

Here's how to draw a cat.

Practice below, because you will need this
skill when you turn the page.

**Can you draw 50 or more cats on these two pages?
How about 100?**

BOXED IN

Can you find the nine-letter words trapped in these boxes? Draw a line from the white starting letter to connect the rest of the letters to form a word. Each letter has to touch the previous letter at a side or a corner. **Answers on page 141.**

This is how you find an earthworm:

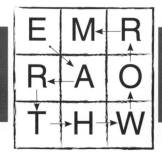

1.

2.

3.

4.

5.

Now try the following puzzles that don't have the starting letters shown, but have clues instead.

6.

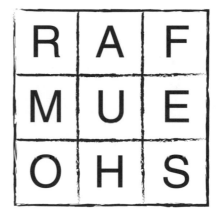

Clue: When he gets dinner, any fin is possible.

7.

Clue: In here, the crowded-in family says "moooove" it.

8.

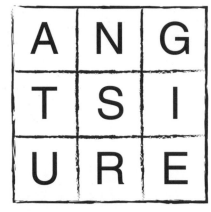

A	N	G
T	S	I
U	R	E

Clue: You place this on the dotted line.

9.

I	R	D
L	F	A
E	G	U

Clue: Don't go swimming without this.

10.

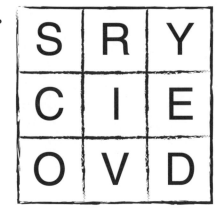

S	R	Y
C	I	E
O	V	D

Clue: Columbus made one of these.

Can you make some of your own Boxed In puzzles?

1.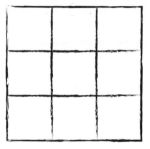

Clue:_____

2.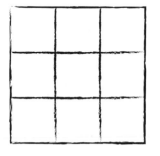

Clue:_____

3.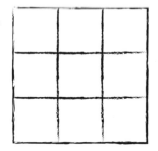

Clue:_____

4.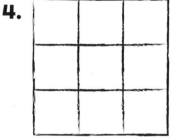

Clue:_____

5.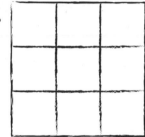

Clue:_____

6.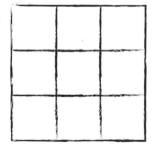

Clue:_____

7.

Clue:_____

8.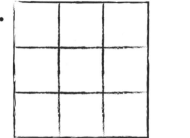

Clue:_____

NO STRINGS ATTACHED

A harp usually has around 47 strings.
Can you add that many and more to the one below?

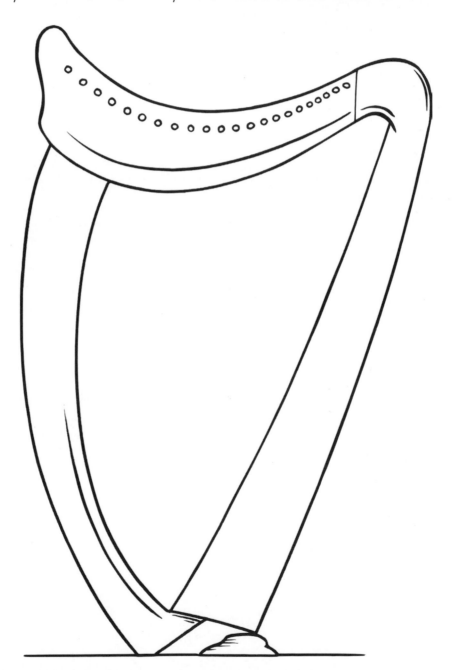

This harp guitar actually exists, and it has 42 strings.
How many can you place?

CURVY...

Can you draw a person or animal using only curvy lines?
What else can you draw using only curvy lines?

Here's more room for your curvy artwork.

FICTIONARY

Can you come up with your own imaginary definitions for these real-but-weird words? Can you also create sentences featuring these words? *Real definitions on page 141.*

1. Lollygag

_____

_____

_____

_____

2. Snickersnee

_____

_____

_____

_____

3. Cabotage

_____

_____

_____

_____

4. Gardyloo

_____

_____

_____

_____

5. Badmash

_____

_____

_____

_____

6. Smellfungus

_____

_____

_____

_____

7. Fartlek

_____

_____

_____

_____

8. Bumfuzzle

_____

_____

_____

_____

9. Oocephalus

_____

_____

_____

_____

10. Godwottery

_____

_____

_____

_____

11. Hobbledehoy

_____

_____

_____

_____

12. Pettifogger

_____

_____

_____

_____

13. Blatherskite

_____

_____

_____

_____

14. Slangwhanger

_____

_____

_____

_____

15. Bawbee

_____

_____

_____

_____

16. Wabbit

_____
_____
_____
_____

17. Cattywampus

_____
_____
_____
_____

18. Erf

_____
_____
_____
_____

19. Collywobbles

_____
_____
_____
_____

20. Loblolly

_____
_____
_____
_____

CHANGE THE SEASONS

Can you change winter to summer?

47

PAIR 'EM UP

Salt and pepper, Jack and Jill. Some things are just made to go together. How many perfect pairs can you think of? List them below. To make it a game, have someone else do the same thing. Then compare lists and cross out any pairs you have in common. The person with the most pairs left over, wins.

UPSIDE DOWN IS RIGHT-SIDE UP

Think you can't draw? You might have better luck if what you're drawing is upside down. Turn this book sideways and try drawing the item below.

Once you're done, turn the book around to see how you did. You might surprise yourself!

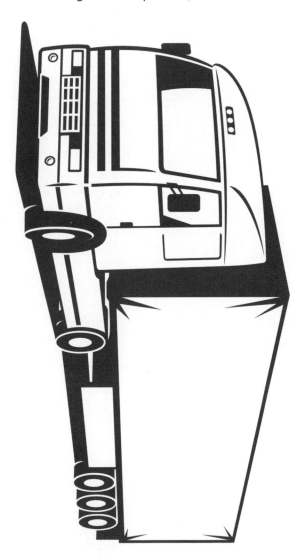

Can you draw this upside-down car? Turn the book sideways and give it a shot.

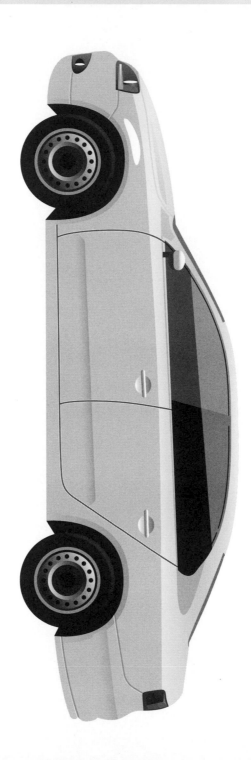

PFWEROUL BIRAN

Can you read the paragraph below?
See page 141 if you're having trouble.

If yuo cna raed tihs, yuo hvae a sgtrane mnid. Olny smoe plepoe can. Aoccdrnig to rscheearch at an Elingsh uinervtisy, it deosn't mttaer in waht oredr the ltteers in a wrod are, the olny iprmoetnt tihng is taht the frist and lsat ltteres are in the rghit pcleas. The rset can be a toatl mses and you can sitll raed it wouthit porbelm. Tihs is bcuseae we do not raed ervey lteter by isltef but the wrod as a wlohe.

This paragraph and others like it go viral every now and then—supposedly proving that the order of letters within words is not important to understanding them as long as the first and last letters of each word are in their proper places. Can you read the following?

1. All wrok nad no paly mkaes Jcak a dlul byo. All paly and no wrok mkaes Jcak a mree tyo.

_____

_____

_____

2. Yuo cna ccath mroe feils wtih hnoey tahn you can wtih vaeingr.

_____

_____

_____

3. Yuo cna laed a hsroe to weatr, but yuo cna't mkae hmi dnrik.

_____

_____

_____

4. A ltlite lnnireag is a duoranegs tnhig.

_____

_____

_____

5. It is btteer to be sarmetr tahn yuo aapepr tahn to aapepr sarmetrr tahn yuo aer.

_____

_____

_____

6. Good tihgns cmoe to toshe woh wiat.

_____

_____

_____

7. An alppe a dya kpees teh dtcoor aawy.

_____

_____

_____

8. An oinon a dya kepes enyrveoe aawy.

_____

_____

_____

9. Dno't cuont yuor cihkencs borefe tehy hcath.

_____

_____

_____

10. Yuo cna't ulbmarcsne a srmacbled geg.

_____

_____

_____

Now, can you come up with some of your own word scrambles for your friends to figure out?

1. _____

_____

2. _____

_____

3. _____

_____

4. _____

_____

5. _____

_____

6. _____

_____

7. _____

_____

8. _____

_____

9. _____

_____

10. _____

_____

MARKING BOOKMARKS

Can you design and create bookmarks for the following types of readers?

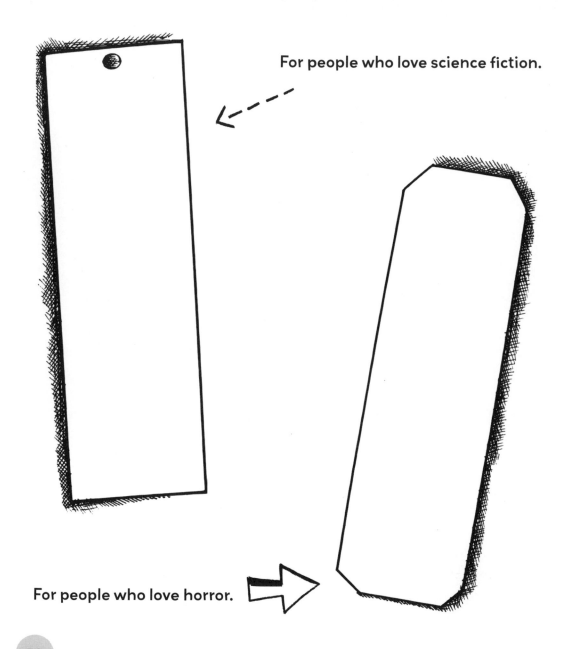

For people who love science fiction.

For people who love horror.

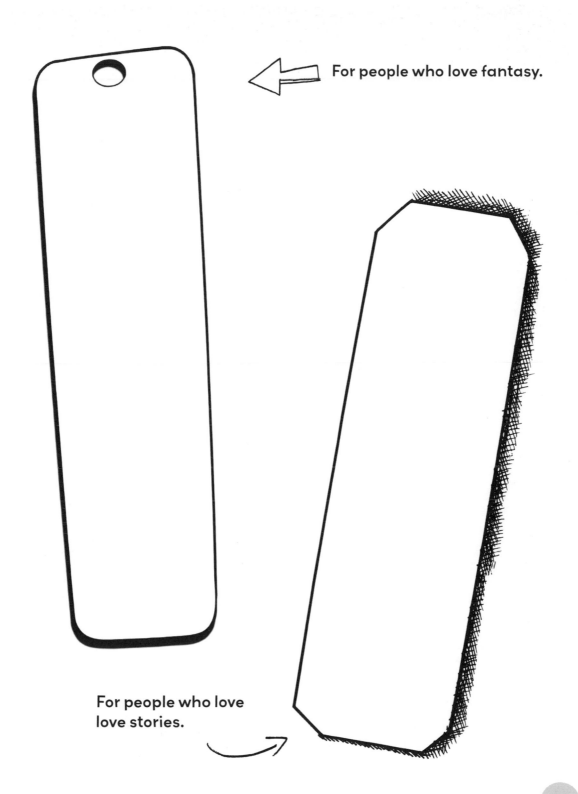

For people who love fantasy.

For people who love
love stories.

For people who love animal stories.

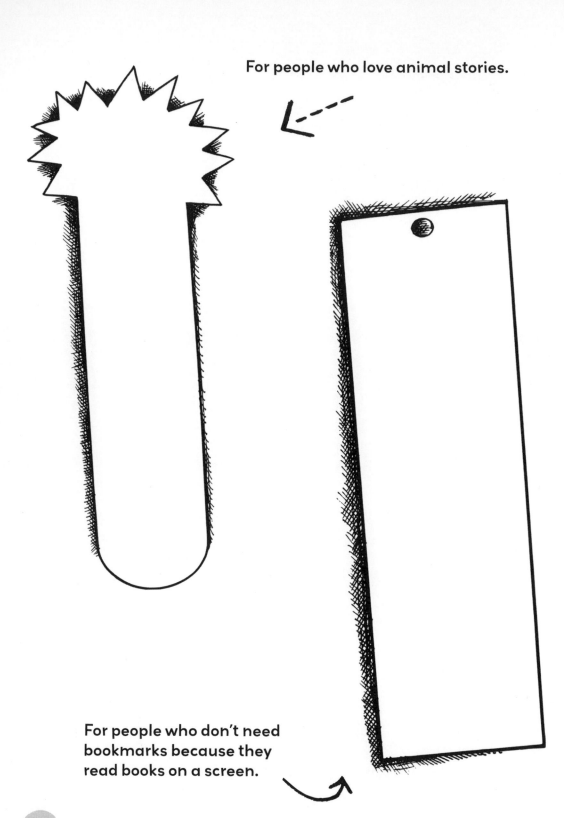

For people who don't need
bookmarks because they
read books on a screen.

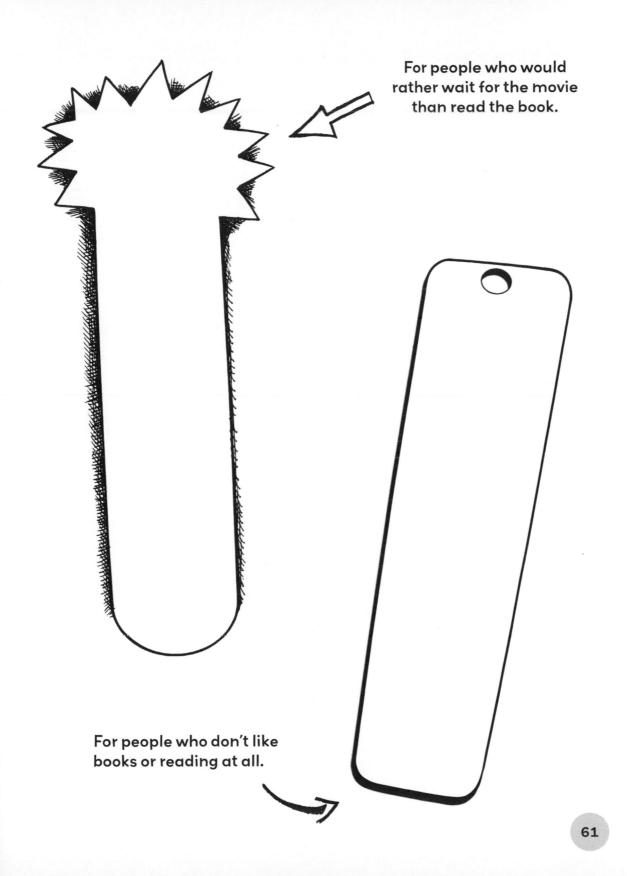

For people who would rather wait for the movie than read the book.

For people who don't like books or reading at all.

61

Here are a bunch of noses. Can you give them funny faces?

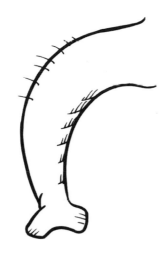

PROVERB COMPLETION

A proverb is a short — usually well-known — statement that expresses a truth. Can you match up the 25 proverb beginnings and endings? **Answers on page 141.**

IS WORTH TWO IN THE BUSH

beggars can't

comes around

DON'T MAKE A RIGHT

A WATCHED POT

A BIRD IN THE HAND

but prepare for the worst

a picture is worth

be choosers

a rolling stone

an island

actions speak louder

flock together

A THOUSAND WORDS

AND YOUR ENEMIES CLOSER

gets the grease

the early bird

when the going gets tough

by its cover

birds of a feather

catches the worm

you can't judge a book

has a silver lining

fortune favors

LAUGHTER IS

hope for the best

than the sword

keep your friends close

should not throw stones

PEOPLE WHO LIVE IN GLASS HOUSES

SPOIL THE BROTH

never look a gift horse

than words

GOOD THINGS COME

to those who wait

every cloud

the best medicine

without breaking a few eggs

THE SQUEAKY WHEEL

gathers no moss

TWO WRONGS

never boils

too many cooks

IN THE MOUTH

YOU CAN'T MAKE AN OMELET

the bold

the tough get going

what goes around

the pen is mightier

no man is

WHAT'S THE POINTILLISM?

Can you create the following items using only dots?

House, Dog, Tree, Woman, Man, Elephant, Truck, Skyscraper, Lamp, Guitar... and whatever else you can think of.

Here's more room for your dotty artwork.

HEART IT

Can you doodle 50 things that
you think are absolutely fabulous?

ALPHA-SENTENCES

Can you write a paragraph in which each word begins with a consecutive letter of the alphabet?

For instance:
Any bear could develop ear frame galoshes...

Write your paragraph here:

A_____ B_____ C_____ D_____ E_____
F_____ G_____ H_____ I_____ J_____
K_____ L_____ M_____ N_____ O_____
P_____ Q_____ R_____ S_____ T_____
U_____ V_____ W_____ X_____ Y_____
Z_____ .

Can you write one sentence in which each word begins with a consecutive letter of the alphabet?

A_____ B_____ C_____ D_____ E_____
F_____ G_____ H_____ I_____ J_____
K_____ L_____ M_____ N_____ O_____
P_____ Q_____ R_____ S_____ T_____
U_____ V_____ W_____ X_____ Y_____
Z_____ .

Can you do it backwards?

Z _____ Y _____ X _____ W _____ V _____
U _____ T _____ S _____ R _____ Q _____
P _____ O _____ N _____ M _____ L _____
K _____ J _____ I _____ H _____ G _____
F _____ E _____ D _____ C _____ B _____
A _____ .

HINKY PINKIES

A hinky pinky is a riddle that begins with a definition. The answer is a rhyming word combination or phrase that has the same number of syllables. For example:

Large Feline = Fat Cat

Rabbit Comedian = Funny Bunny

Can you complete the following hinky pinkies?

Answers on page 142.

1. A rodent's wife =

_____

2. Gloves for baby cats =

_____

3. A shaky stomach =

_____

4. A small violin =

_____

5. A library thief =

_____

6. A hip ghost =

_____

7. When a bovine steps on your foot =

_____

8. A measurement device for large sea mammals =

_____

9. A pleased father =

_____

10. A flower who lies around all day =

_____

11. Jelly beans at the beach =

_____

12. A lengthy tune =

_____

13. A clean road =

_____

14. Lives in the basement =

_____

15. Place of learning that gives you homework on holidays =

_____

Can you guess these hinky pinky drawings?

16.

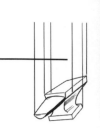

17.

18.

19.

20.

THE NONSENSE BAND

This band is posed without their instruments. Can you draw a completely ridiculous, never-before-seen musical instrument for each band member?

The Nonsense Band has just release their newest CD. Can you design the cover?

There are 12 songs on the new CD. Can you come up with some crazy, nonsense titles for these songs?

1. _____
2. _____
3. _____
4. _____
5. _____
6. _____

7. _____
8. _____
9. _____
10. _____
11. _____
12. _____

Can you design the Nonsense Band's t-shirts, bumper stickers, and buttons?

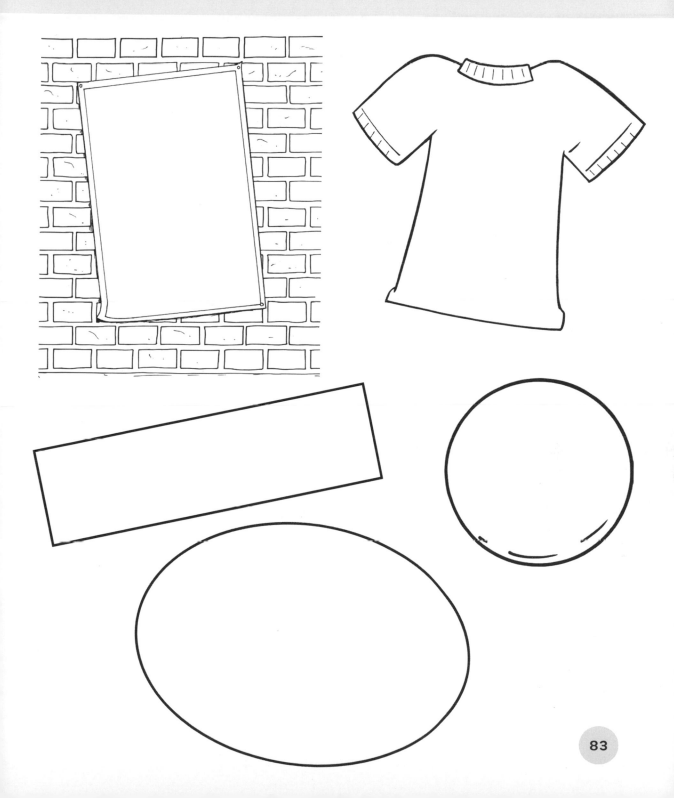

CODE CREATOR

Can you create your own code using symbols? Create a symbol for each letter of the alphabet, and then write a letter to a pet or friend.

G 3 Y K #
4 Z M π
⇨ W 11
@ ℒ 36

A	**B**	**C**	**D**
E	**F**	**G**	**H**

I	J	K

L	M	N

O	P	Q

R	S	T

U	V	W

X	Y	Z

FAST-FOOD THINKING

Can you come up with at least 20 different fast-food restaurants in three minutes? To make it a game, have someone else do the same thing. Then compare lists and cross out any restaurants you have in common. The person with the most restaurants left over, wins.

1._____

2._____

3._____

4._____

5._____

6._____

7._____

8._____

9._____

10._____

11._____

12._____

13._____

14._____

15._____

16._____

17._____

18._____

19._____

20._____

21._____

22._____

23._____

24._____

25._____

26._____

27._____

28._____

29._____

30._____

Here's a page for your friend:

1._____
2._____
3._____
4._____
5._____
6._____
7._____
8._____
9._____
10._____
11._____
12._____
13._____
14._____
15._____

16._____
17._____
18._____
19._____
20._____
21._____
22._____
23._____
24._____
25._____
26._____
27._____
28._____
29._____
30._____

Enter

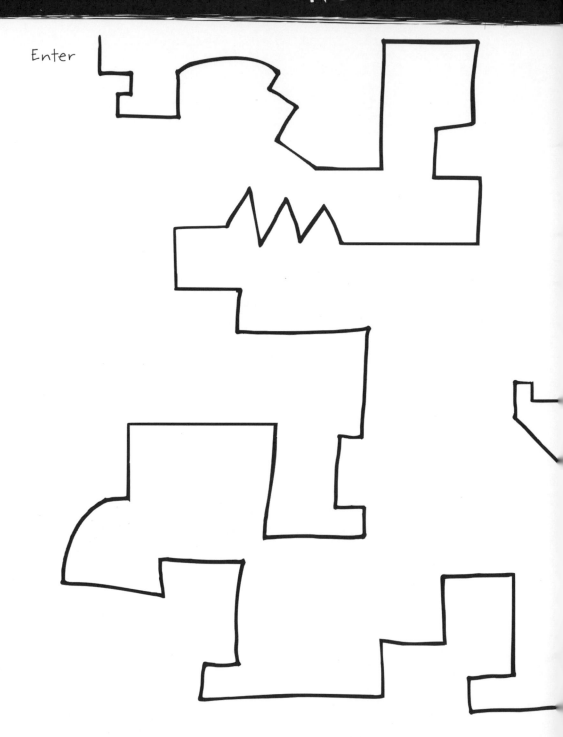

Mazes are a lot of fun to solve, but they can also be a lot of fun to create. The line on these pages is the solution to a maze that has yet to be created. Can you draw it? Make sure to include lots of dead ends.

Exit

SHAPING UP

Can you draw the following shapes without lifting the pencil off the paper AND without retracing any of your lines AND without crossing over an existing line? Hint: for some of these shapes, there is more than one way to do this. **Answers on page 142.**

For example:
One way to draw this shape

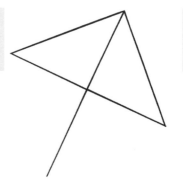

1. without lifting the pencil off the paper
2. without retracing any of the lines
3. without crossing over an existing line

Would be this:

Try other ways of solving this example here:

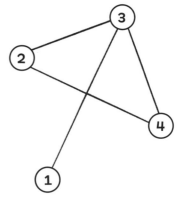

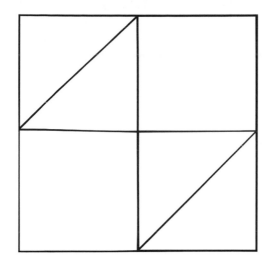

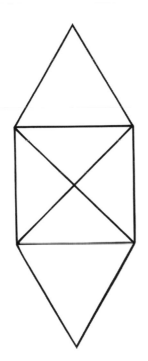

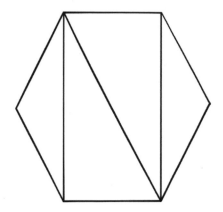

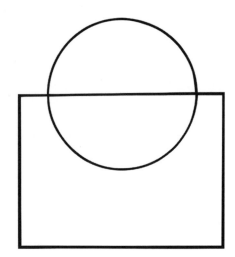

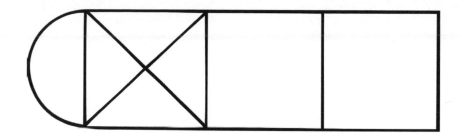

FRAMED!

Can you create a fictional family? Use the photo frames below to "tell a story" of a family from some point in the past all the way up to today.

MORE MIX & MATCH

Following the instructions on page 24, can you connect these illustrations so they spell out compound words? To make this a little more challenging, the answers are mixed in with the clues.
Answers on page 142.

STRAIGHT...

Can you draw a person or animal using only straight lines?
What else can you draw using only straight lines?

Here's more room for your straight artwork.

HCRAES DROW

Can you solve these word-search puzzles in which each of the words are spelled backward? **Answers on page 142.**

```
R T S U G U A F H M H B L
E T P B W M I C L K C Y L
B B R E B M E C E D R E C
M Y A M U I N P Z H A Q U
E I R S Y U U N A E M G F
T U E A S Y J Z E M I E W
P U B L Z K P H V J B Q S
E Z O Q I U C G W R C O P
S I T T Q R I F U V Y Y A
I M C J C L P A T A D L S
C O O L D M R A I P T U M
N P I U N Y R A U N A J F
R E B M E V O N L D B K J
```

Clue: The months of the year

```
R Z U C A N M R X B F M L L
T N A H P E L E K T M L E G
B D Q V V N O I L O K M O J
D I X R F T N I N M U R I W
C V Y L S D V K Z R I I U H
K Y D N K W E E Z L B Q O A
L W A K Q Y M D L R E G I T
U K C L E F F A R I G S A E
E S O R E C O N I H R C L E
A H Q R A E B R A L O P A H
D C U S P X X Z X Z P F O C
W A F Q S P V N Z F Y R K C
W A V K S O D T I O P P I H
A R B E Z I R A E J R N F T
```

Clue: 15 zoo animals

```
R H R M Z K P O X H O I A W Y S L
E S G I K K D N J P J L Q A C P S
I A J E Z I C E E X K H H R K I R
U D Q G H H E R H C C T A H P H E
X R L O S J A V A O Z B B M D S D
D E H Y S T Z N N E B J X Z N E D
L D A S I R D N E L V D B W I L A
C L D O C Y E B E H C L E V M T L
Z A N E L C Y K T V T Y O T R T D
Y B O A T Z E S C C G O O C E A N
T L N F F S W S J E O R G S T B A
L D O I Y R R O S N H S E Q S X S
R U Q P N I A N K F E C T E A K E
R A H M O T M P L N G P A U M S T
S P O A O N Q M K I R F R L O J U
E U Q Z U L O L P R Z S T C M C H
D I X S G J W M L N N V S S E H C
```

Clue: 15 popular board games

```
K X W O B W W B B V J T E E N G Z U Z
B E F A Z J Z S G U R N V G W D U F R
O N N I L O I V R F E N P Z H A L Y N
H O T U U V G T Q V S N N T V U P P Z
S B E S W N U M D B W A U K T B B Y A
O M N O Y L C I C T C B D E I G T O Q
R O I M E E K W W C A P R S Q F E R R
J R R N C N V S O I W R I W M L P S O
H T A G Y P O R X Y G A Q S D S M U L
H V L O F Z D H F U E H H N I F U W L
O I C Y R I Y Z P B W A J P Z M R Y E
C U S P O X W A U O R C Z K D O T R C
E V F N B G A Z N M X U J D F N B A I
D X H U N T Y R O R F A N D Y A H N W
M G A Y V Z G N A E W Q S F A I W D Z
L G W R O O I I K T E K W S Y P R Q P
X W L N K C J X K V I Z Y O U U K T W
D E W P A T R D H N W U Y L M J R V U
N W N N H Z I T V O Y X G S G U J Z L
```

Clue: 14 musical instruments

THE MAP TEST

Can you draw a map of the world from memory?
See page 143 for a map of the world.

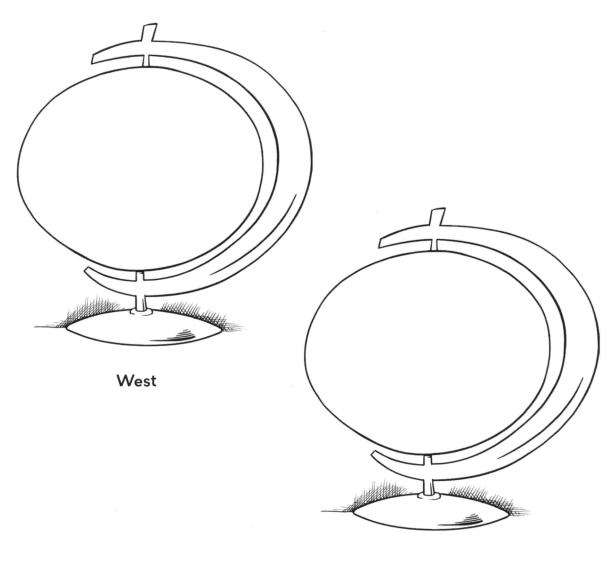

West

East

Can you draw the United States with the 48 continental states? No peeking!
See page 143 for a map of the U.S.

FAST CARS

Can you come up with at least 25 different car makes and models in five minutes? To make it a game, have someone else do the same thing. Then compare lists and cross out any cars you have in common. The person with the most cars left over, wins.

1._____

2._____

3._____

4._____

5._____

6._____

7._____

8._____

9._____

10._____

11._____

12._____

13._____

14._____

15._____

16._____

17._____

18._____

19._____

20._____

21._____

22._____

23._____

24._____

25._____

Here's a page for your friend:

1._____

2._____

3._____

4._____

5._____

6._____

7._____

8._____

9._____

10._____

11._____

12._____

13._____

14._____

15._____

16._____

17._____

18._____

19._____

20._____

21._____

22._____

23._____

24._____

25._____

WITHOUT A CLUE

Can you solve these crossword puzzles without any clues?
Answers on page 144.

The Continents

Which day of the week is missing from this puzzle? _____

Can you come up with your own mini crossword puzzles on this page?

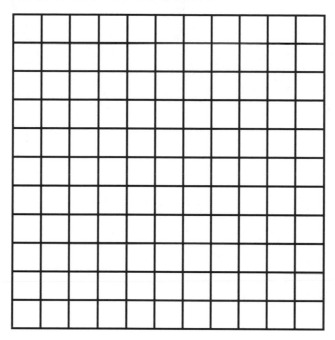

Theme: _____

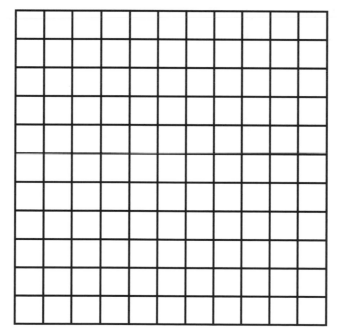

Theme: _____

H8 IT!

Can you doodle 50 things that you think are absolutely horrible?

ALPHABET SOUP

Can you draw at least 100 letters to make a
yummy alphabet soup?

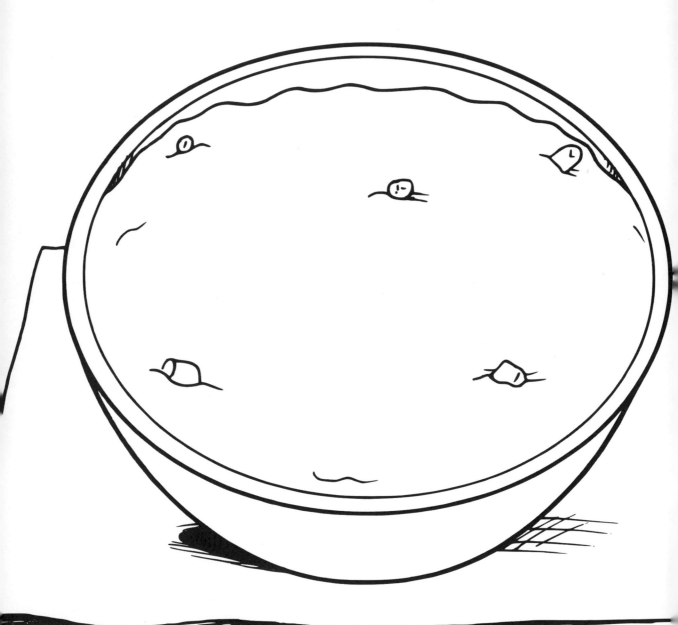

RUBBER DUCKIES

Here's how to draw a rubber ducky:

Practice below, because you will need this skill when you turn the page.

Can you fill the tub with at least 50 rubber duckies?

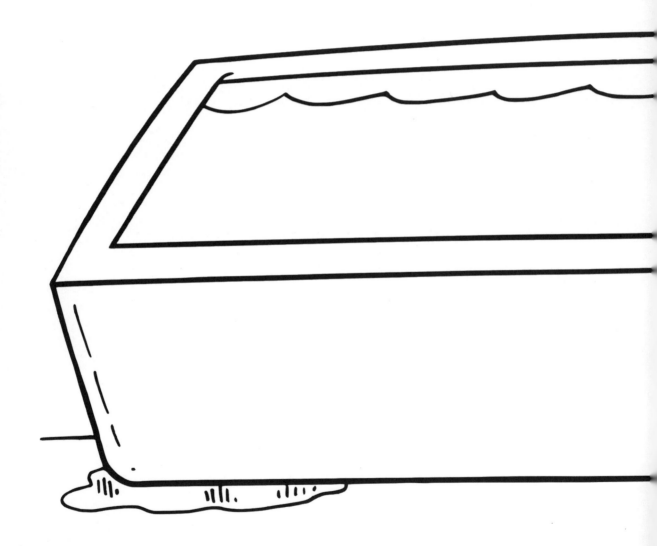

A PERSON OF FEW WORDS

Can you tell your life story using only six words? Six-word memoirs became an Internet phenomenon a while back, which started when SMITH magazine hosted a contest. Use the space below to try out different words and sentences until you're down to six words. For an example, here is mine (the author of this book!): Creates fun activities. Sits all day.

As you're writing, try not to overthink it. You can be serious, silly, sarcastic, or even just random. Ask everyone around to give it a try and write what you all come up with below.

_____

_____

_____

_____

_____

Can you write a six-word description of your latest family vacation?

_____

_____

_____

Can you write a six-word history of your school lunch cafeteria?

_____

_____

_____

Can you tell us about your best friend in six words?

_____

_____

_____

How about a six-word memoir about a pet?

_____

_____

_____

Or your favorite actor?

_____

_____

_____

Can you write a six-word short story?

_____

_____

_____

Can you create a six-word horror story?

_____

_____

_____

Or a six-word love story?

_____

_____

_____

How about a six-word story about a mad scientist?

_____

_____

_____

CONNECT THE DOTS

Can you connect all nine dots using only four straight lines? You cannot pick up your pencil and each dot can only be touched once. **Answer on page 144.**

Now, can you connect all nine dots using only THREE straight lines? You cannot lift your pencil from the page and you cannot cross any line already drawn. Answer on page 144.

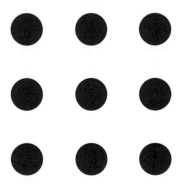

Can you connect the 15 dots with six straight lines that are joined and do not cross each other? Answer on page 144.

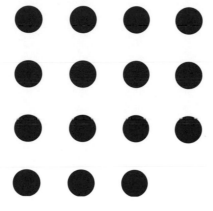

ALL T E PRESIDE TS

Can you find all the presidents from George Washington to Barack Obama in the word search puzzle on the next page?
Answers on page 144.

- -

George Washington
John Adams
Thomas Jefferson
James Madison
James Monroe
John Quincy Adams
Andrew Jackson
Martin Van Buren
William Henry Harrison
John Tyler
James Polk
Zachary Taylor
Millard Fillmore
Franklin Pierce
James Buchanan
Abraham Lincoln
Andrew Johnson
Ulysses S. Grant
Rutherford Hayes
James Garfield
Chester Arthur
Grover Cleveland

Benjamin Harrison
William McKinley
Theodore Roosevelt
William Taft
Woodrow Wilson
Warren Harding
Calvin Coolidge
Herbert Hoover
Franklin D. Roosevelt
Harry S. Truman
Dwight Eisenhower
John F. Kennedy
Lyndon Johnson
Richard Nixon
Gerald Ford
Jimmy Carter
Ronald Reagan
George H. W. Bush
Bill Clinton
George W. Bush
Barack Obama

```
C L A J I N K R N T A N D R E W J A C K S O N U J E J H T C
A B R A H A M L I N C O L N K W K H H N N K J L M G P N U K
L J O H N Q U I N C Y A D A M S G H J O W O W A A Q K C W R
V G P B G U V K H N H H T T H O M A S J E F F E R S O N O M
I R U T H E R F O R D H A Y E S W I E Z S Q H C X S F K O F
N N P T K I X H X H S N I S B H R I C H A R D N I X O N D U
C J J N L F P R U O B B G R R N G J J G E R A L D F O R D
O H N J T U M T B T X X N O A O Y E M A R U K V H M J J O T
O Q W F J F F W N I N I L H S R P O P M G P W I H A A C W N
L A Y N Z Q H I Z B D Y Y I E D X R H E O W J O Q R M H W G
I A X D O E L U V R A R R W Y E R G A S Z I S K F T E D I S
D S L I G C W Q A T N R O A U F T E R M U L P E R I S P L U
G E J R L R Z H Y E A H A Q W L L W R A L L B G A N B G S F
E N O L M U N R H H N F X C E X P B Y D Y I R N N V U W O O
V E I Y R E A M N E E Z M V K F Z U S I S A O F K A C G N N
G B S O R H A I S E K N E X Y O X S T S S M N U L N H H Y B
V K D R C I M I A D L S A P S J B H R O E M A R I B A X U J
Q T A A L A E E C P O R J V S K W A U N S C L Z N U N S B A
Y W Z L J T G H O O J J A G H O J D M T S K D T P R A W J N
O F I N H D I F R V Y G W Z I D K M A A G I R J I E N I I D
J W E G R O V E R C L E V E L A N D N L R N E A E N Z L M R
T B I H G K R T P M D T J J S P S Y M Q A L A M R X I L M E
N W C G J O H N A D A M S O E H V K V N N E G E C U A I Y W
D O M F D X B H E R B E R T H O O V E R T Y A S E C H A C J
R L X O G E O R G E W A S H I N G T O N J V N M K S E M A O
C H E S T E R A R T H U R M K A T J A M E S P O L K E T R H
D H M I L L A R D F I L L M O R E Y D G A Z E N H Z E A T N
T E L Y N D O N J O H N S O N A T K L P E Y G R Y B X F E S
F R A N K L I N D R O O S E V E L T W E Z Z F O A J L T R O
J O H N F K E N N E D Y X J A M E S G A R F I E L D M B M N
```

SUPER FAST HEROES

Can you come up with at least 25 different superheroes in three minutes? To make it a game, have someone else do the same thing. Then compare lists and cross out any superheroes you have in common. The person with the most superheroes left over, wins.

1._____

2._____

3._____

4._____

5._____

6._____

7._____

8._____

9._____

10._____

11._____

12._____

13._____

14._____

15._____

16._____

17._____

18._____

19._____

20._____

21._____

22._____

23._____

24._____

25._____

26._____

27._____

28._____

29._____

30._____

Here's a page for your friend:

1._____

2._____

3._____

4._____

5._____

6._____

7._____

8._____

9._____

10._____

11._____

12._____

13._____

14._____

15._____

16._____

17._____

18._____

19._____

20._____

21._____

22._____

23._____

24._____

25._____

26._____

27._____

28._____

29._____

30._____

YOU CAN PUN BUT YOU CAN'T HIDE

Can you fill in the blank with the appropriate pun?
Answers on page 144.

For example:

At karate today, Pig practiced his **pork chop.**

1. A fake noodle is sometimes called an im _____.

2. A lazy kangaroo is called a _____ potato.

3. Did you hear about the guy whose whole left side was cut off? He's _____ now.

4. Pizza makers with flour on their face at the end of the day have a 5 o'clock _____.

5. You can tune a guitar but can you _____ fish?

6. They spelled his name wrong on his tombstone. It was a _____ mistake.

7. What did the raisin say to his mother? "You did a _____ job raising me."

8. The baby duck cried because he wanted a snack but they were all out of

_____ers.

9. What did the healthy bucket say to the sick bucket? "You look a little

_____."

10. Why didn't the cyclist enter the unicycle race? He was two

_____.

11. I forgot how to throw a boomerang, but it _____.

12. What do you need when you're dehydrated? A _____ aid kit.

13. I took the shell off my racing snail, but he just got more _____ish.

14. A bear with no teeth is a _____ bear.

15. If you tell too many bad jokes, you will be _____ished.

PICTURE THIS

Can you complete the following sentences with drawings and doodles instead of words? **Answers on page 144.**

1. [blank box] -lieve in yourself.

2. [blank box] love you!

3. The [blank box] -erpillar soon became a butterfly.

4. I h- [blank box] you loud and clear.

5. I can't [_____] to see you sick like this.

6. Billy [_____] a ghost last night.

7. That baby is just so a- [_____] -able.

8. [_____] you hold your breath for two minutes?

The Answers

The Bicycle Test (page 6)

It All Adds Up Answers (page 8)

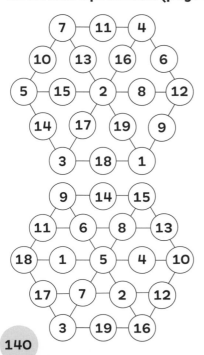

Gridlock Answers (page 12)

A-4; B-16; C-12; D-9; E-20; F-24; G-14; H-21; I-3; J-10; K-25; L-5; M-13; N-1; O-19; P-8; Q-22; R-18; S-7; T-26; U-15; V-23; W-2; X-17; Y-6; Z-11

A. I always thought air was free ... until I bought a bag of chips.
B. Adults are just kids with money.
C. You're so old that when you were a kid, the Dead Sea was only sick!
D. Be yourself; everyone else is already taken.
E. Why do cows wear bells? Their horns don't work.
F. Can February March? No, but April May.
G. What would you call the child of a vampire and a snowman? Frostbite!

Six Answers, Three Clues Answers (page 21)

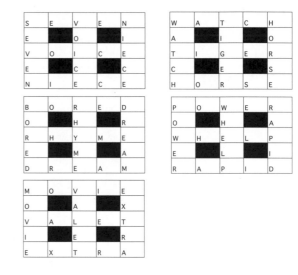

Mix & Match Answers (page 24)

Arm + Pit = Armpit
Box + Car = Boxcar
Cow + Boy = Cowboy
Jig + Saw = Jigsaw

X Marks the Spots Answers (page 28)

Boxed In Answers (page 32)
1. Dragonfly; 2. Cornflake; 3. Education;
4. Mousetrap; 5. Dangerous; 6. Fisherman;
7. Farmhouse; 8. Signature; 9. Lifeguard;
10. Discovery

Fictionary Answers (page 42)
1. Lollygag: To move slowly
2. Snickersnee: A long knife
3. Cabotage: The right to operate sea, air, or other modes of transportation within a territory
4. Gardyloo: An old warning shouted before throwing waste from a window
5. Badmash: Naughty
6. Smellfungus: A pessimist
7. Fartlek: A training technique for long-distance runners
8. Bumfuzzle: To confuse someone
9. Oocephalus: A person or animal with an egg-shaped head
10. Godwottery: Nonsense
11. Hobbledehoy: An ill-mannered boy
12. Pettifogger: A lawyer who argues over unimportant matters
13. Blatherskite: A person who talks a lot without making much sense
14. Slangwhanger: A loud, abusive speaker
15. Bawbee: A Scottish coin
16. Wabbit: Exhausted
17. Cattywampus: Askew or awry
18. Erf: A plot of land in South Africa
19. Collywobbles: a stomachache
20. Loblolly: A North American pine tree with long, slender needles

Pfweroul Biran Answers (page 54)
If you can read this, you have a strange mind. Only some people can. According to research at an English university, it doesn't matter in what order the letters in a word are, the only important thing is that the first and last letters are in the right places. The rest can be a total mess and you can still read it without problem. This is because we do not read every letter by itself but the word as a whole.

1. All work and no play makes Jack a dull boy. All play and no work makes Jack a mere toy.
2. You can catch more flies with honey than you can with vinegar.
3. You can lead a horse to water, but you can't make him drink.
4. A little learning is a dangerous thing.
5. It is better to be smarter than you appear than to appear smarter than you are.
6. Good things come to those who wait.
7. An apple a day keeps the doctor away.
8. An onion a day keeps everyone away.
9. Don't count your chickens before they hatch.
10. You can't unscramble a scrambled egg.

Proverb Completion Answers (page 66)
A rolling stone gathers no moss
Laughter is the best medicine
A bird in the hand is worth two in the bush
What goes around comes around
Every cloud has a silver lining
Two wrongs don't make a right
The pen is mightier than the sword
The squeaky wheel gets the grease
When the going gets tough the tough get going
No man is an island
Fortune favors the bold
People who live in glass houses should not throw stones
Hope for the best but prepare for the worst

Good things come to those who wait
Birds of a feather flock together
Keep your friends close and your enemies closer
A picture is worth a thousand words
You can't judge a book by its cover
The early bird catches the worm
Never look a gift horse in the mouth
You can't make an omelet without breaking a few eggs
A watched pot never boils
Beggars can't be choosers
Actions speak louder than words
Too many cooks spoil the broth

Hinky Pinkies Answers (page 76)
1. Mouse spouse; 2. Kittens' mittens;
3. Jelly belly; 4. Little fiddle; 5. Book crook;
6. Cool ghoul; 7. Ow, cow; 8. Whale scale;
9. Glad dad; 10. Lazy daisy; 11. Sandy
candy; 12. Long song; 13. Neat street;
14. Cellar dweller; 15. Cruel school;
16. Pig jig; 17. Splat cat; 18. Star car;
19. Number slumber; 20. Icicle bicycle

Shaping Up Answers (page 94)

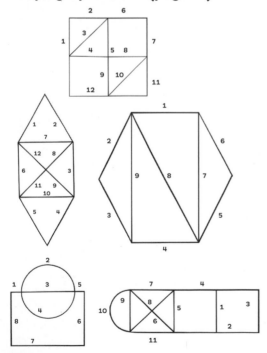

More Mix & Match Answers (page 102)
Pig + Tail = Pigtail
Bag + Pipes = Bagpipes
Bar + Code = Barcode
Break + Dance = Breakdance
Ear + Phone = Earphone

hcraeS droW Answers (page 108)

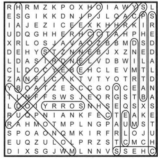

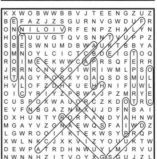

The Map Test Answers (page 112)

Without a Clue Answers (page 116)

Connect the Dots Answers (page 130)

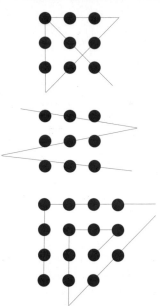

You Can Pun But You Can't Hide Answers (page 136)

1. Pasta; 2. Pouch; 3. All right;
4. Shadough; 5. Tuna; 6. Grave; 7. Grape;
8. Quack; 9. Pail; 10. Tired; 11. Came
back to me; 12. Thirst; 13. Slug;
14. Gummy; 15. Pun

Picture This Answers (page 138)

1. Bee; 2. I; 3. Cat; 4. Ear; 5. Bear; 6. Saw;
7. Door; 8. Can

All the Presidents Answers (page 132)

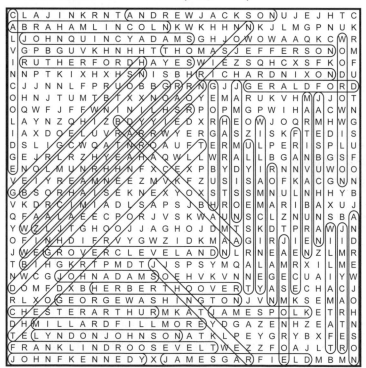